your guide to moving to secondary school

"My older sister used to tease me about how I would be the smallest in the school. It wasn't until I got there on the first day I really believed her – everyone was massive, I felt like a toddler walking through a jungle of people knees."

"I don't think I quite understood how different it was going to be. I had the usual crisps for morning break in my bag, as well as a tennis ball to play with in the non-existent playground!"

"There was a rumour that on the first day some new boys were put in the school dustbins. I spent the day in terror, fearing that I would end up in the bin. What a relief when the final bell went!"

Scripture Union England and Wales, 207–209 Queensway, Bletchley, MK2 2EB, England.
www.scriptureunion.org.uk

First published 2000, revised 2003, 2005, 2007

ISBN 978 1 84427 212 9

British Library Cataloguing-in-Publication Data
A catalogue record for this book is available from the British Library.

Cover and internal design by David Lund Design
www.davidlund-design.com

Printed and bound in by Nuffield Press, Abingdon.

With special thanks to Tim Cutting of the Bridgebuilder Trust, Nick Jeffery of Norfolk YMCA and Scripture Union schools workers.

This book was given to

Ross James

By: St Paul's Church, Parkend

In preparation for secondary school

Date: 17 July 2007

My personal profile

Name

Date of birth

Height (without heels!)

Primary school

Favourite subject

Favourite teachers

Best friends

Secondary school

Form tutor

First day of term

Collect **the signatures** of people you want to **remember!**

(and phone numbers!)

A-Z survival guide

Arguments Moving schools can be a stressful time, so you are quite likely to lose your temper or get irritable. You may argue with your parents about your school uniform, or with old friends at school who are not spending so much time with you. If you're getting wound up, count to ten before you say anything, or walk away.

Assemblies Like them or hate them, assemblies have to happen! In your new school they will probably be shorter and less fun. Some assemblies will include prayers or times of quiet. Use that opportunity to think about what was said and to think quietly or maybe pray for yourself and others.

Boys (for girls!) There could be plenty of new boys to get to know and if you're a girl (and not going to a girls-only school!) that might be good or bad news! Some boys want to show off and many will seem immature. But others will be worth getting to know as friends. It's not worth trying to get a boyfriend too quickly – having lots of friends is much more fun!

Books

There are plenty of books and some will be great! The school library is a good place for homework or finding out information. Try to read what you need for each lesson and find good books that'll help with your studies and your life.

Idea: You might even want t see if the world's best selling book has anyth to say! (See page 63 to out what it is.)

Bullying

Bullies are weak people. There's no excuse for bullying. If you think you're being bullied, don't let it go on. Tell a teacher, or another adult you can trust, immediately. That's the brave way to deal with cowards. Page 23 gives you some wise advice on this!

Break

A great time to let off steam, but takes some getting used to in a larger school. Try to stick with friends and stay in one place for a few days, until you feel confident to move around and mix a bit.

Brothers and sisters in school ...

If you have a brother or sister who is already at your new school, it can either be great, or pretty embarrassing! Teachers may read the list of names in the class and ask, "You're not related to HIM/HER, are you?" in a worried voice! They may expect you to be the super-human creep that he or she is. Don't worry – just be you, not anyone else.

"I remember being horrified when I went into the toilets and saw my rebellious sister's name all over the walls!"

Canteen

Moving to secondary school can mean you have a better choice of food at lunchtime. But when loads of young people get together to eat, it can be very noisy. If you use the dining room, watch what everyone else does. And try not to drop your tray on the first day!

Choices You will have to make choices about many different things, including the friends you have, clubs you join, sports you play, or even the kind of lunch you eat! Later, you will have to choose subjects which could affect your future. Of course, there are also important choices to do with right and wrong. To make choices you need guidance, so talk to teachers, parents and friends. Many people ask God to help them make the right decisions.

Clubs There will be plenty of clubs at your new school – chances to play more sport, make music or develop other interests. Make the most of these opportunities, but don't take on too much. You'll need time and energy for your home life and social life. Some schools have a Christian Union, which is a lunch-time or after-school club where young people go to find out more about God. You may think the CU is going to be boring or full of odd people. You may be wrong, but you'll never really know until you try!

Detention Some schools keep students in at lunch-time or after school if they forget homework or break school rules. Detention is a waste of everyone's time, so it's best to keep out of it. If you do end up in detention, try to behave, or you'll end up in another one.

Drugs Illegal drugs are bad news. There may be a few students who want to persuade others to use drugs. They are always expensive and always harmful. It may be tempting to experiment, but drugs can cause illness and long-term problems and cause users to lose control of themselves. If you come across them at school, walk away and report it – you'll be saving others from pain as well as yourself.

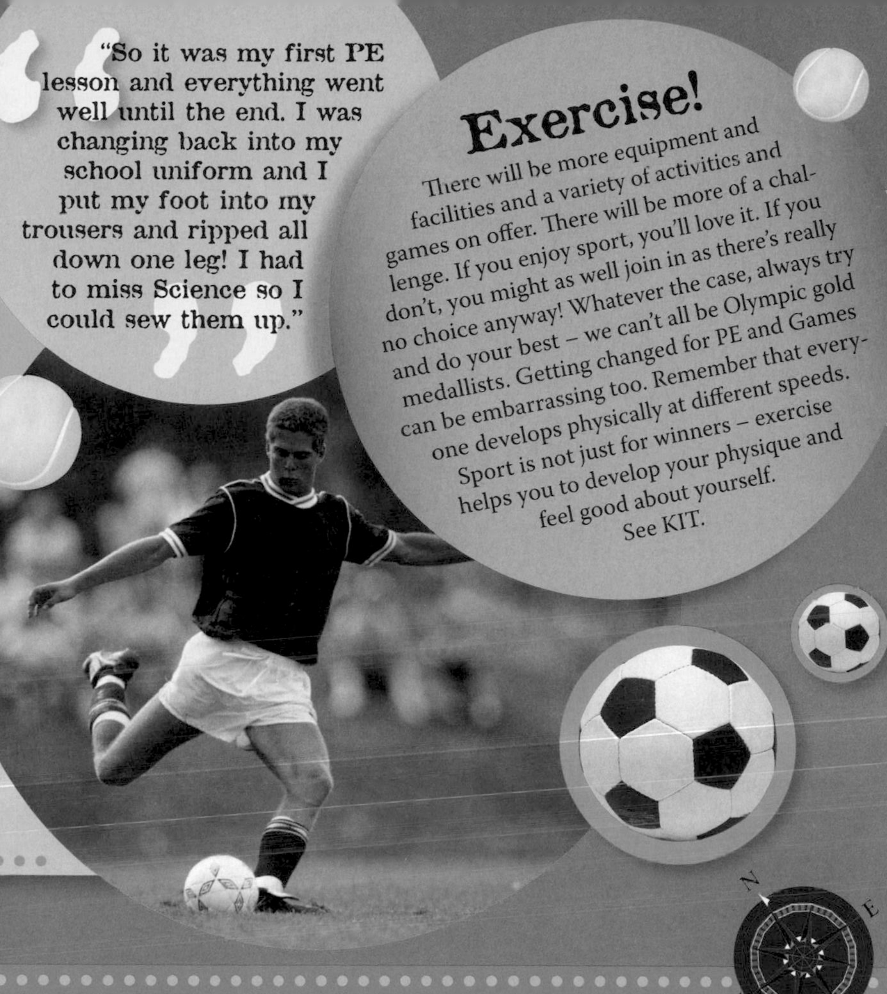

"So it was my first PE lesson and everything went well until the end. I was changing back into my school uniform and I put my foot into my trousers and ripped all down one leg! I had to miss Science so I could sew them up."

Exercise!

There will be more equipment and facilities and a variety of activities and games on offer. There will be more of a challenge. If you enjoy sport, you'll love it. If you don't, you might as well join in as there's really no choice anyway! Whatever the case, always try and do your best – we can't all be Olympic gold medallists. Getting changed for PE and Games can be embarrassing too. Remember that everyone develops physically at different speeds. Sport is not just for winners – exercise helps you to develop your physique and feel good about yourself. See KIT.

Finding your way

Even if you do get lost, it's not the end of the world. If you can, use a map of the school, even if it is confusing! By the end of the first week, you'll know your way around. Always ask someone where you should go, rather than stumbling into a class of Year-10s! And try not to get separated from others in your class – then you can all get lost together!

Form tutor This is the teacher who checks the register and deals with any problems. Form tutors are usually chosen carefully because they are approachable and helpful. Don't be afraid to tell them if things are going wrong or if you feel bad about your first days at the school. They really are there to help.

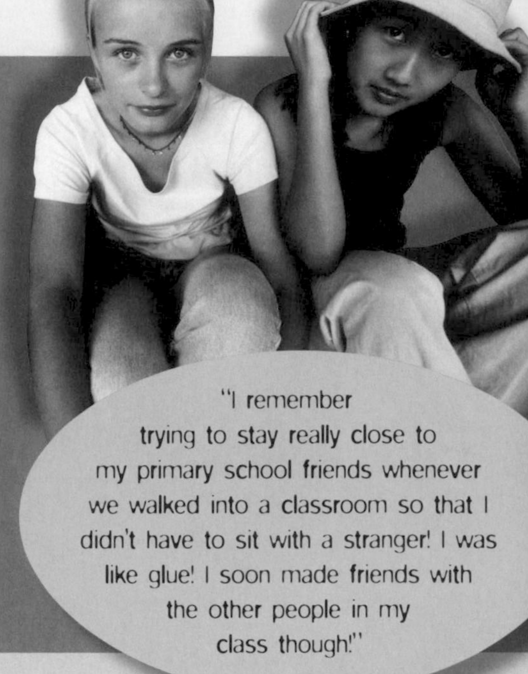

Friends

If your friends are not going to the same school, you may feel a bit lost and lonely. But you won't be the only one. And friends from your old school may suddenly decide they've had enough of you as a friend! Very soon you'll probably find someone who has got things in common with you and a new friendship begins. If you make the effort to talk to others who seem to be on their own, you will find yourself making friends. Write a list of new friends after two weeks and see how well you have done.

"I remember trying to stay really close to my primary school friends whenever we walked into a classroom so that I didn't have to sit with a stranger! I was like glue! I soon made friends with the other people in my class though!"

Girls (for boys!)

Being in larger, mixed schools usually brings boys into contact with more girls. That can seem wonderful! Often, however, most of the girls in the school will be older than you and most will not want to have anything to do with you. Try to get to know girls as friends and keep the friendships you had with the girls in your old school. Don't worry about getting your own 'girlfriend' yet. There's enough to get used to being in a new school without all that!

Heads

There are heads of subjects, heads of year, deputy heads, and the feared or famed head teacher! All these teachers have special roles in school. They make sure you all learn and do well. Don't be scared of any of them! Tell them about anything that worries you.

HOMEWORK

There's no escape! Homework can be interesting, but it usually takes time. Get into the habit of doing it as soon as you get home and hand it in on time. Leave it too late and it can be hard to catch up.

Use the homework timetable on page 62. Homework is really important – it may mean learning, completing exercises or writing notes. Your next lesson will usually follow on from the homework you've done.

Induction day

This is a really important day for you. Turn to page 61 for the induction day checklist!

Journey Your school journey may be much longer and you're more likely to go by public transport. Allow enough time to get there in your first week. Being late will get you noticed for the wrong reasons. If you are late, give the honest reason why – teachers have heard all the false excuses before. On the school bus, you may think there's no one to sit next to. But after a few days you're likely to have friends to sit with. The same is true if you walk to school. You'll meet up with others going the same way.

"I remember there were no seats left on the bus, so I had to stand. It moved off really quickly and I fell over in front of everyone!"

Kit Remember when you need your PE or Games kit and make sure they are clean enough. There may be some kind of penalty at school if you don't have the correct kit at the correct time. So it is worth sorting out a routine right from the start. See PE and GAMES.

Loos School toilets are not always the cleanest or most private places in the world! Make sure you discover where they are on your induction day and use them for what they were intended – and nothing else. They are not a good place to hide from lessons, as in most schools they are regularly visited by staff. ("So where is a good place?" we hear you cry. Well, we're not telling you!)

"Before starting at secondary school, I was worried about making new friends, finding my way there, finding all my different classes, even finding the loos! I didn't go to the loo at school until my fourth day!"

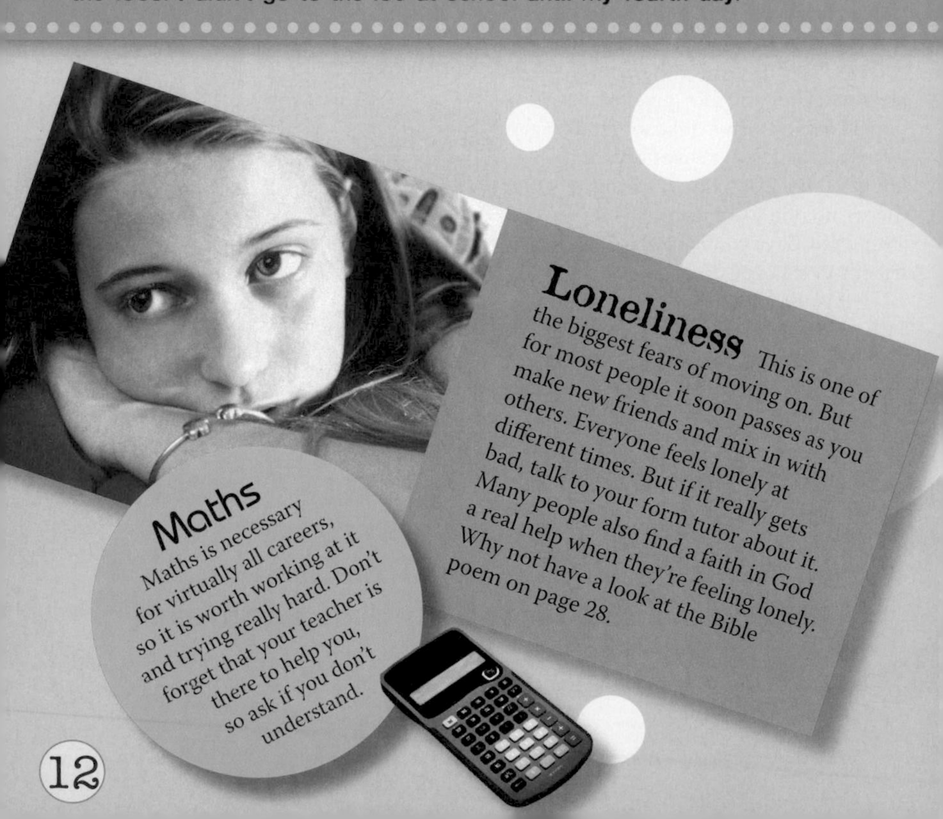

Loneliness This is one of the biggest fears of moving on. But for most people it soon passes as you make new friends and mix in with others. Everyone feels lonely at different times. But if it really gets bad, talk to your form tutor about it. Many people also find a faith in God a real help when they're feeling lonely. Why not have a look at the Bible poem on page 28.

Maths Maths is necessary for virtually all careers, so it is worth working at it and trying really hard. Don't forget that your teacher is there to help you, so ask if you don't understand.

Money You'll find that you will always feel like you need more money than you actually have. But money is not always available, so decide what you really need and what you don't. You need money for lunch and bus fares, but don't take too much in case you lose it or it gets taken.

New You will look and act 'new' for a few days. Starting somewhere new does give you a chance to put the past behind you and make a fresh start. If you start really well, you won't have to 'catch up' later on. Your new school is a great opportunity to make a positive new beginning. First impressions are important.

Office The school office is a busy place, with the staff doing many jobs. Once you get used to the way the school office works, you will be confident about how to use it and how the staff can help you. Most office staff are very friendly!

Parents Despite being so old and out of touch, parents do want to know how their kids are getting on. They want you to succeed and be happy. If you're not, they will worry. Try to let them help you by talking to them about the good things and the hard things too. If you are finding it really hard, ask them to speak to school for you. See page 22.

PSHE and Citizenship

Personal, social and health education (PSHE) covers a range of subjects looking at how you develop as a person. It includes health, relationships and sex, developing confidence and making the most of your abilities. Through PSHE you should learn that it is OK to be different and have beliefs which others don't share. Citizenship helps you become an informed and active citizen in our society, looking at things such as the law and police, social issues and politics.

Quiet people

It's great that we're all different! Some people seem quiet; others really loud. Many quiet people are thinkers who don't say much but listen to louder people making fools of themselves! There is nothing wrong with being quiet. Sometimes people are loud because they're nervous or insecure. And if you are more of an extrovert, just be yourself. But don't forget to be sensitive to others. Quiet people also make good friends because they listen to your problems.

Religious Education (RE)

Faith, religion and spirituality are as vital to people as the question of their roots or history. It is important to understand different faiths, and how they influence attitudes and behaviour. You will explore different religions, beliefs, values, and ceremonies, and learn to respect others. Christians believe in God and follow his ways, as shown in the Bible. They believe that Jesus came to show us what God is like and to show us how God wants us to live our lives.

RULES

All schools have rules and sanctions. Most are for the safety and well-being of all the students. You may even get a chance to create your own form rules. Rules are there to follow rather than to break. Find out what they are and stick to them from the start. If you don't, you may find yourself with things like detentions, report cards and letters home to your parents… not a good start!

Size

Look around the hall, full of all the new pupils. You'll see some boys and girls who look almost fully grown, and others who are still really small! Everyone develops at a different rate. If you are smaller or less physically developed, don't worry. You'll have your growth spurt.

"I remember standing with all the other 'newies' on my first day and feeling incredibly short! My dad told me that one day I'd catch everyone else up – and I did!"

Teachers

You are likely to have many more teachers, with a different one for every subject. Some teachers seem less friendly than others, but don't let that put you off their subject. Teachers are there to help you learn, so ask them questions or tell them if you don't understand things. Try to remember that teachers are normal people, with problems and moods just like you!

Tests and exams

Tests and exams are part of school life. As you get older they will help you decide what you are good at and what you may want to do in the future. All you can do is your best. You will do better if you've prepared for them and you don't panic.

Timetable

Your new school timetable tells you what subject you do, where and at what time. It may seem complicated, but as long as you copy it down correctly it will soon make sense.

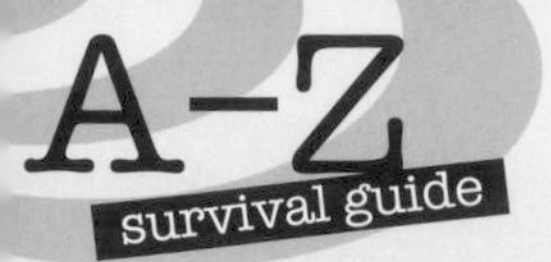

Uniform

Your new school uniform may be more formal and strict than you are used to. Schools usually have uniforms to make the students feel united and look moderately smart. The rules will be clear on what you can and can't wear.

Website

Many larger schools now have their own websites and many of the questions you would like to ask will be on it. There may also be more up-to-date information than in the prospectus, with news about school trips, sports competitions and staff changes. Websites are a great way to access information, so it is well worth a look.

Youngest

Being the youngest in school (and possibly the smallest) could make you feel vulnerable and scared. By this time next year, however, you'll feel settled and confident, while next year's newest pupils will be feeling as you do now.

"I was too scared to ask where my next lesson was so ended up getting shouted at because I just stood in the corridor and was late. (It was Maths, so can you blame me?!)"

Zits

The time you change school coincides with adolescence, when you and your body are changing. Zits, spots or acne (whatever you call them) are unavoidable as you grow up. Try not to pick spots as this will spread the infection from one area to another. A few people may suffer really badly, but a doctor should be able to offer some help if this is the case.

Top ten answers

781 children in the United Kingdom, who are about to move on to secondary schools, were asked these three questions. Their answers make up the top ten charts on the next few pages.

- What is the best thing about your new school?
- What will you miss most of all about your old school?
- What is the most scary thing about your new school?

How would you answer these questions? Turn over to see if your answers are in the Top Ten! Here are comments from three children in Bolton.

"On the visit, I liked my form tutor and getting things to do in geography. But I disliked some older children because they pushed me in the ice-cream queue! I want to be in the school football team. My dream is to be a footballer."

"I'm looking forward to my new school because it's bigger and it's got more rooms and I'll get a different teacher for every lesson. I wouldn't like it if I didn't make any friends. I'm looking forward to playing either a cornet or a trumpet, and after-school clubs. When I get older, I would like to be a lawyer and drive a silver Jaguar."

"I like my new secondary school because it's got interesting sports. I can't find anything I dislike except for the fact that it's falling apart! On my visit I did rock-climbing and abseiling. That was fun. I also met some teachers. They were kind. I want to become either a policeman, a lawyer or a pilot."

Thanks to the children from Balvanich Primary (Isle of Benbecula); Cairnshill Primary (S Belfast); Coppull St John's Primary (Lancashire); Gibson Primary (Omagh); Gilnow Primary (Bolton); Hillview Primary (Hucclecote, Gloucester); Kingsland School (Bangor, N Ireland); Loughton Middle School (Milton Keynes); Mellor Primary (Leicester); many Nottinghamshire Primary Schools who know Nick Harding!; St Anthony's RC Primary (Watford); St John's C of E Primary (Sparkhill, Birmingham); St John's C of E Primary (Brinscall, Lancashire); St John's C of E Primary (Whittle-le-Woods, Lancashire); St Joseph's RC Primary School (Carryduff, N Ireland); St Mary's C of E Primary (Kirtbury, W Berks); Swanbourne House School (Milton Keynes).

What is the best thing about your new school?

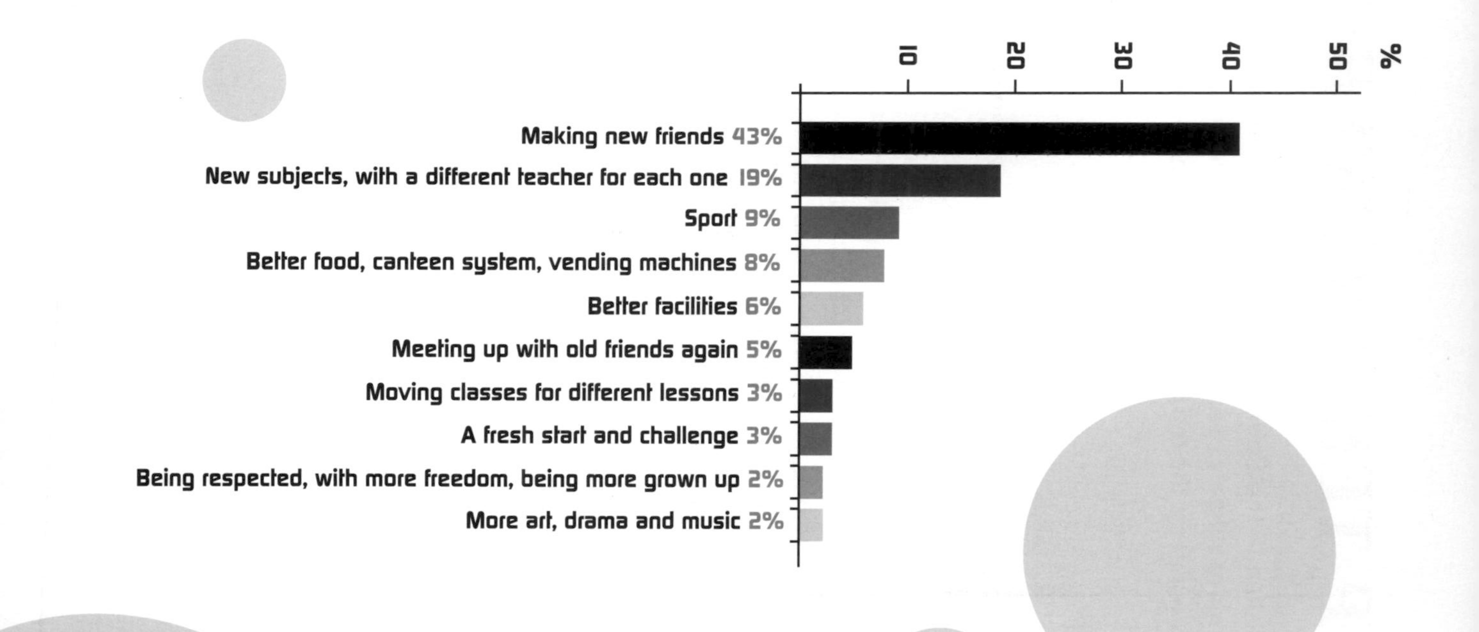

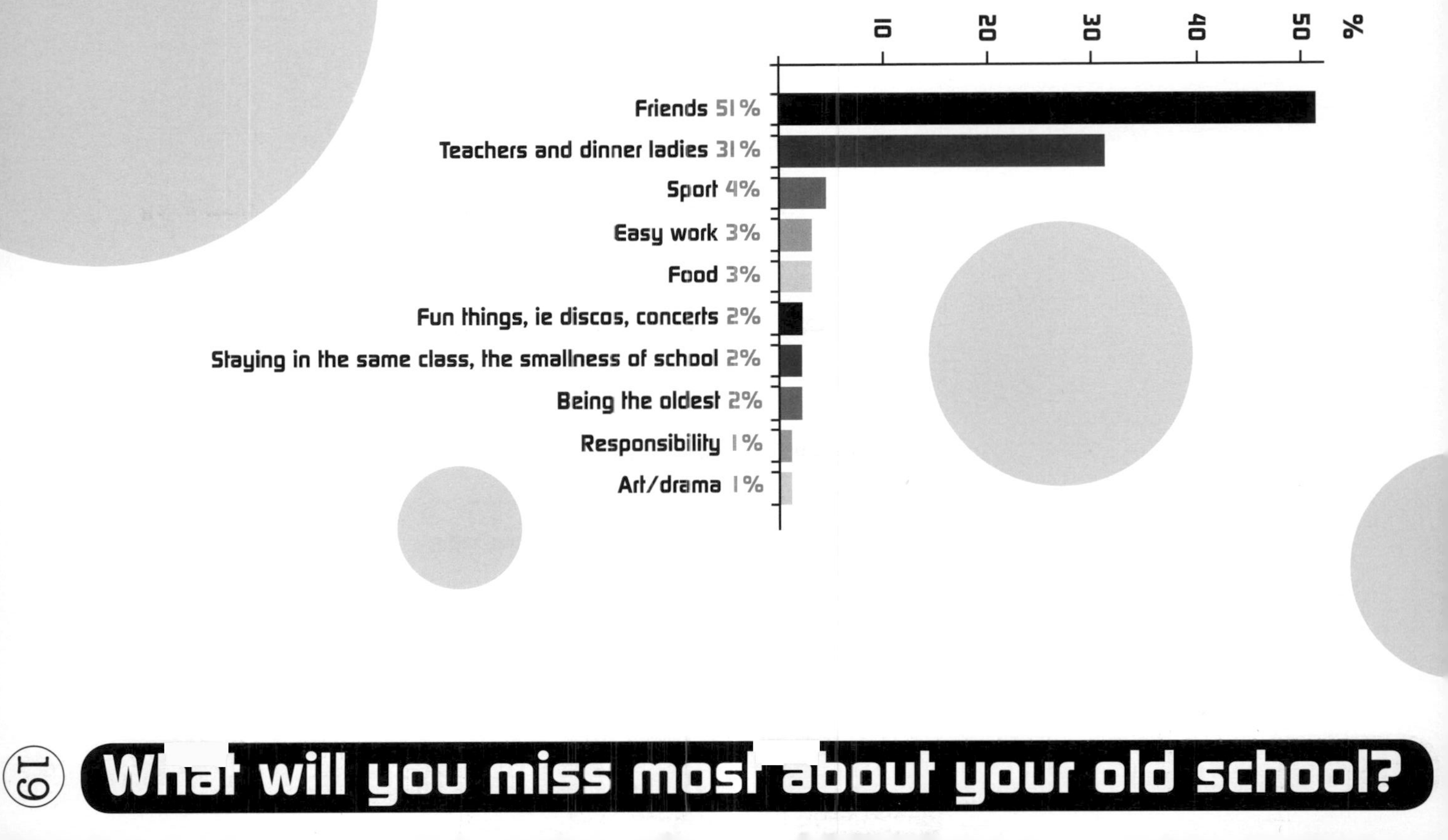

What will you miss most about your old school?

What is the most scary thing about your new school?

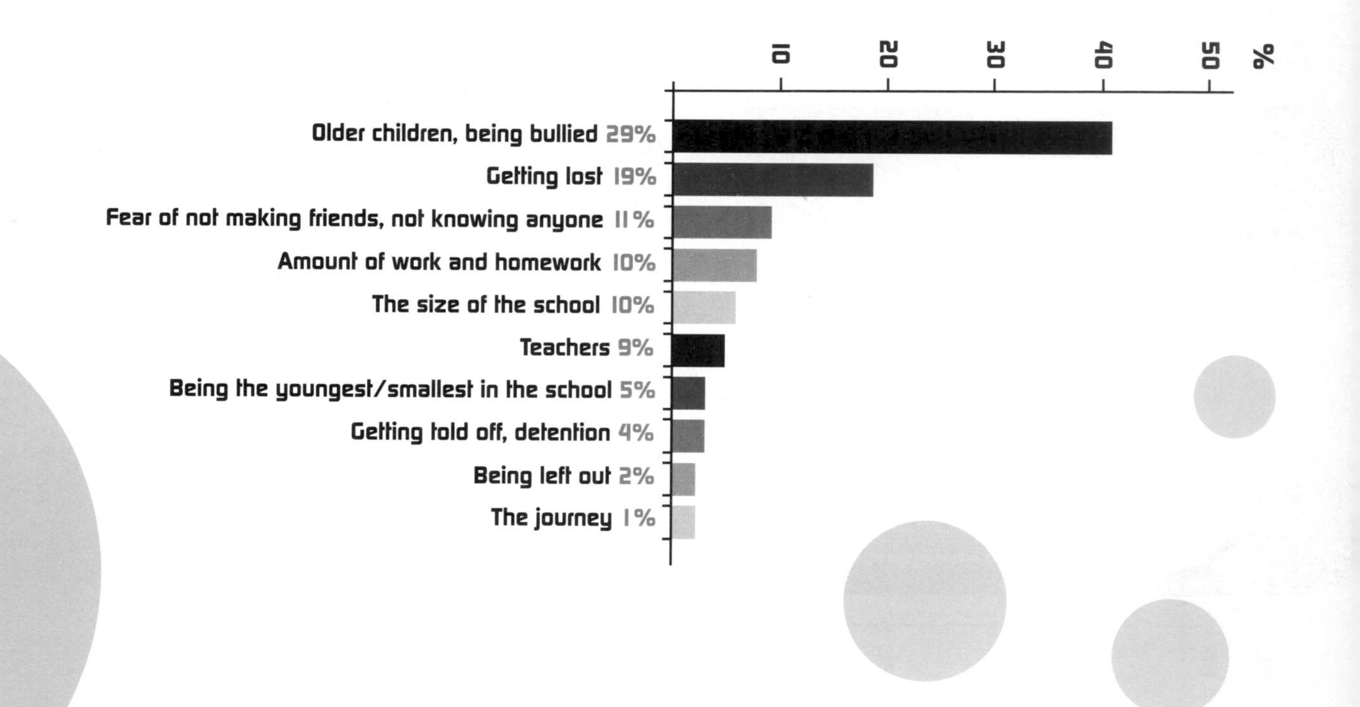

Friends

Friends are like fire,

spreading across vast areas

and reaching out for everything in its path.

But when something new and different comes along – like water,

it can all extinguish with one blast

so your friendship is left as history, as ash.

But sometimes there's a spark.

If you save that spark,

you can light it again.

Your friendship can start again,

slowly return to what you had.

You're still you

You're swapping your recorder for a rock guitar
You've put a centre parting in your hair.
You've thrown away those CDs with the nice songs on,
And black's the only colour that you'll wear.

You look at me as though I'm sad, or even worse,
As though I'm getting past my sell-by date.
You need me as your taxi-driver every night,
But you don't want me at that new school gate.

But you're still you and I'm still me,
Just two people getting by.
Making our way in this world so wide,
Can we still walk side by side?

OK, so I'm your mother and right down deep
Are some complicated feelings for you.
I want you to be happy and I know I can't keep
You a child for ever. What should I do?

So let me go slowly, tell me I'm cool,
That we're just two people finding a way
To pass through changes in this world so wide
And still walk side by side.

Can we still walk side by side?

Gill wrote this when her daughter, Emma, was about to move to Impington Village College in Cambridge.

What shall I do? HELP!

Nick Jeffery spends his time in Norfolk 'helping boys and girls settle into their secondary schools'. He's met thousands of people who know about bullying, which is one of the things that can really worry you when you change school. If you need convincing, look at the questionnaire results on page 20. He's worth listening to:

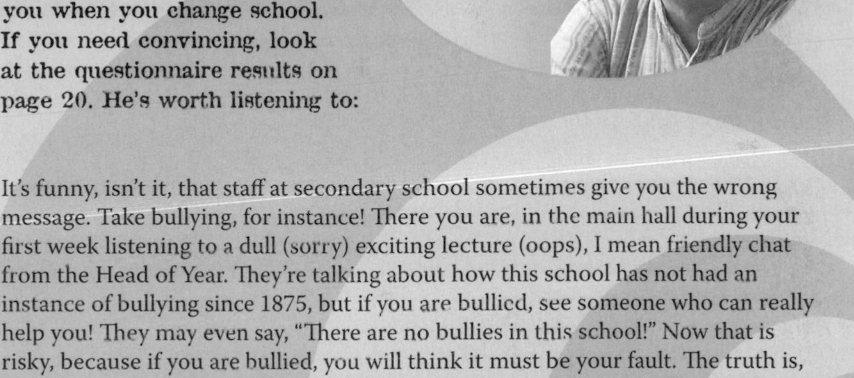

It's funny, isn't it, that staff at secondary school sometimes give you the wrong message. Take bullying, for instance! There you are, in the main hall during your first week listening to a dull (sorry) exciting lecture (oops), I mean friendly chat from the Head of Year. They're talking about how this school has not had an instance of bullying since 1875, but if you are bullied, see someone who can really help you! They may even say, "There are no bullies in this school!" Now that is risky, because if you are bullied, you will think it must be your fault. The truth is, every school has bullies. If you think about it, I bet you've been bullied before. And if you're really honest, you've probably bullied someone yourself too! (Yes, even someone as angelic as you!) Believe it or not, being bullied is not the real problem; it's what you do about it that counts.

There is an unwritten rule in school amongst pupils that says, "Never tell on a bully!" Why not? Who says? Doesn't it just make things worse, mess up the victim's life and make the bully think they can get away with it? Or have I missed the point? Being bullied can make us feel really lonely. Some pupils won't tell anyone at all. They just stay silent and suffer. There is an episode of *The Simpsons* – you know, the one where Nelson is bullying Bart. He is being 'got' after school. He sits in the classroom all day, terrified but not doing anything about it. At the end of school he tries to run away but Nelson is waiting and beats him up. Nelson tells him that he will get beaten up every day after school! Eventually Bart does something about it.

What would you do? Have a look at 'Dilemmas' and see how you get on...

Dilemmas ??

1. Your mate is being pushed around by some big kids and calls to you for help. What do you do?

A Pretend you didn't hear anything and scurry off to your next class. ○
B Dive in, like Superman, to the rescue only to limp out five minutes later with more than your pride hurt. ○
C Ask an adult in school to sort it out. ○

2. Someone in your tutor group has started picking on you and has threatened to beat you up after school. What will you do?

A Spend all day worrying about it instead of concentrating on your lessons, and pray that they will forget. ○
B Face the bully and threaten them with worse stuff. ○
C Wait for the end of tutor time, then quietly explain what is going on to your tutor or an adult you trust. ○

3. Your friend rushes into the tutor group, late. There's a long piece of loo paper hanging out of the back of his trousers. Do you...

A Fall about in hysterics, with everybody else? ○
B Drag him outside before anyone sees? ○
C Report it so that the teacher can deal with this serious matter? ○

4. In Science, you overhear two of your tutor group whispering about a secret you shared with just your best friend. What will you do?

A Say nothing and stop being best friends. ○
B Make up some things about your friend and tell everyone to get your own back. ○
C Confront your friend, hear their side of the story, then decide what to do. ○

5 You find some kids in the toilets, blocking the sinks and turning on the taps. They see you and tell you to ignore it, "or else!" Do you...

A Ignore it? ○
B Stop the flood by unblocking the sinks yourself? ○
C Find an adult immediately? ○

How did you get on?

Mostly A
OK, so you like to play it safe, but watch out. You may become a doormat or you could be in danger of being bullied yourself. You have rights and are special. Try to be more like C.

Mostly B
Woah! You throw caution to the wind and get stuck in there. Slow down, take a deep breath and think before you act or you could find yourself in big trouble at school.

Mostly C
You're not scared to speak out about what's going on around you. Once a bully sees you can't be intimidated, they'll soon give up. But you don't have to report everything to a teacher. Some things you can deal with yourself – like stray loo paper!

So, was it as bad as you expected?

Jonathan Hulin

was a bit scared he'd have the mickey taken out of him because he hated sports – all sports – but especially football. Also, because he was tall and skinny, he dreaded the communal showers. He suffered agonies just thinking about it.

"It was hard at first. Some people used to call me names like 'Twiglet' and stuff, but my real friends stuck by me. I played football because I had to but, by the end of the autumn term, I realised I didn't hate it any more. I actually looked forward to it. And now that I play regularly, I'm not so skinny any more. I've got muscles!"

Sophie Friend

had mixed feelings about going up to secondary school.

"I was scared that I might not make any friends and that I'd get bullied, though I was excited too because it was such a big step in my life."

So, how did Sophie survive? Did she make friends? You bet she did. Her social diary is currently booked solid and she's having the best time ever!

Danielle Wade

was worried about her speling, sorry, spelling! She thought the teechers would get mad at her for making misteaks.

Did they? "No, they were really nice. They kept giving me commendations to encourage me. I got bundles of them. In Year 7 you've only got to blow your nose and someone will give you a commendation for it. But make the most of it. They don't bother once you get into Year 8!"

Geoff Miller

thought he'd keep getting lost when he started senior school. It was humungous; ten times bigger than his primary school:

"It was like a maze. Endless corridors, hundreds of rooms, thousands of people. But it was fine because in Year 7 all my lessons were in the same rooms. I never got lost once. And now I know my way around the whole school."

Come to the edge

Come to the edge.
We might fall.
Come to the edge.
It's too high!

Come to the edge
And they came
and he pushed
and they flew.

This poem was quoted by Mary McAleese in her inaugural address as the President of the Irish Republic, when she was urging people to take risks and to trust.

You notice everything I do!

You notice everything I do!

You have looked deep into my heart, Lord,
and you know all about me.
You know when I am resting and when I am working,
and from heaven you discover my thoughts.

You notice everything I do and everywhere I go.
Before I even speak a word
you know what I will say
and with your powerful arm
you protect me from every side.
I can't understand all this!
Such knowledge is far above me.

Where could I go to escape
from your Spirit or from your sight?
If I were to climb up to the highest heavens,
you would be there.
If I were to dig down to the world of the dead
you would also be there.

Suppose I had wings like the dawning day
and flew across the ocean.
Even then your powerful arm
would guide and protect me.
Or suppose I said, "I'll hide in the dark
until night comes to cover me over."
But you see in the dark

because daylight and dark are all the same to you.

You are the one who put me together
inside my mother's body,
and I praise you
because of the wonderful way you created me.
Everything you do is marvellous!
Of this I have no doubt.
Nothing about me is hidden from you!

I was secretly woven together
deep in the earth below,
but with your own eyes
you saw my body being formed.
Even before I was born, you had written in your book
everything I would do.

This poem is actually taken from a book called the Bible and can be found in a section called Psalms (psalm means 'song'). Life is like a book, made up of many chapters. In your life, the previous one is about to end and the next one is about to begin. And it is a very important one. You are in for big, big changes. All the future lies ahead. But, at the same time, you can't help thinking about the past.

King David, who probably wrote this poem, knew all about making big mistakes in the past and he knew all about getting worried about the future too. But what stopped him from getting overwhelmed and creeping into a corner to hide was that he knew God was with him everywhere he went and whoever he was with. That's not a scary thought because there was no need to try to hide from God. After all, God knew all about him, even from before he was born. He knew how David would turn out and would protect him. David's life was so full of adventures that he certainly needed that protection!

David was a king who lived nearly three thousand years ago. But what he said about God then is still true! People who read David's songs and poems in the Bible have always loved Psalm 139. They know God notices everything about them and wants the very best for them. It's true for you too, as you begin the next chapter of your life.

doooooo

OK – we know that you love doodling on your school-books so here's a place where you can doodle to your heart's content without getting told off. Why not get your best friends to draw a cartoon of themselves to remind you of them when you move on to your next school?

doooooo

oodling

oodling

Mega wordsearch

Can you find all these words in the grid?

Secondary
Timetable
School
IT
CD ROM
Bus
Classroom
Teacher
Canteen
Trainers
Homework
Friends
Exam
Uniform
Pen
Ruler
Tutor
Book
Library
Art
Maths
PE
Chips
Form
SATS

T	I	M	E	T	A	B	L	E	T
E	C	D	R	O	M	K	J	U	R
A	X	R	U	L	E	R	T	I	A
C	L	A	S	S	R	O	O	M	I
H	A	B	M	A	R	W	P	R	N
E	L	N	U	T	E	E	B	O	E
R	I	O	T	S	P	M	O	F	R
O	B	F	O	E	C	O	O	I	S
M	R	O	F	H	E	H	K	N	N
M	A	T	H	S	C	N	I	U	E
F	R	I	E	N	D	S	L	P	P
A	Y	R	A	D	N	O	C	E	S

Sheep's eyeballs

By Robert Harrison

It was the stewed eyeballs that did it. Daniel had been thinking that he might enjoy life at the king's school in Babylon, but as those sheep's eyes floated away from his disgusted gaze, he realised that there were some things he would never get used to. He fought the powerful urge to vomit and longed to be back home in Jerusalem, at his old school, with his own friends. Oh, for a bowl of mum's chicken soup! But there was no going back.

Daniel was a Jew, from the holy city of Jerusalem. Jerusalem had been destroyed by the King of Babylon, and Daniel had been hand-picked for a royal education at the king's private school.

"Eat it!" commanded the harsh voice of the chief steward, frantically waving a long wooden cane at Daniel.

Daniel said nothing. He let the revolted look on his face speak for itself. Out of the corner of his eye, he saw a slave girl, about his own age, delivering fresh fruit along the line of seated students. The prospect of eating fruit had never been more appealing.

"If you do not eat," the old steward said pompously, "you insult the king!"

Daniel had picked up the basics of the Babylonian language on his lonely journey from Jerusalem, and asked, "Why?"

"Your food comes from the king's own table," the wrinkled Babylonian insisted. "Whoever rejects the king's food, rejects the king; and whoever rejects the king…" The steward drew his cane dramatically across his throat, leaving Daniel in no doubt that rejecting the king was not something anyone did twice.

"I imagine that his royal highness, the king, will be enjoying the finer cuts of these sheep," Daniel said politely, pointing to the floating eyes.

His suggestion was met with wide-eyed disbelief. "This," the steward's cane trembled above Daniel's silver bowl, "is one of Babylonia's greatest delicacies. I," he rapped the cane proudly on the floor, "have never had the honour of eating 'enlightenings'."

Daniel slumped over the revolting supper.

"Eat it!" the steward ordered again.

The man strutted away, his cane tapping the floor as he went. Daniel watched as the next student laughed together with the chief steward. The steward and the student turned towards Daniel and smiled. Daniel looked quickly down at the five rubbery balls floating in a sea of blood and wine in his bowl.

What should he do?

It wasn't just Daniel's stomach that shouted at him not to touch the food; his brain and his deepest emotions were also screaming at him. No self-respecting Jew would ever eat such a thing. The Jewish people had clear rules, directly from God, saying, "Don't do it!" Daniel was caught between the orders of the king, and those of God.

The slave girl with the fruit was getting closer.

Daniel knew that at least three other Jews had been sent to the royal school. But they had all travelled separately and he didn't know who they were. He looked up and down the dining hall at his fellow students, each seated crossed-legged on a flat cushion, all presented with the same vile delicacy – 'enlightenings'. Further along this long line, he spotted another face that was twisted with disgust. Its owner looked like a Jew. Daniel wondered if students were allowed to talk to each other during meals. Everyone was seated alone, so it appeared not.

He watched and waited. He needed someone talk to, someone like him, someone who would understand why he could never eat food like that.

The other Jew – if he was a Jew – was cautiously dipping some bread into the spaces between the sightless, floating eyes. Daniel picked up his own loaf of royal bread but did not dip it in his bowl; eating blood was also strictly forbidden to Jewish people.

The fruit girl had reached the student next to Daniel. She wore the white tunic of a junior slave, which contrasted with her skin – a rich, beautifully dark colour. He wondered where her home had been, and whether her city had been destroyed, like Jerusalem. When she came to Daniel, she bent low to deliver the fruit, and whispered, "Eat up, eat up. Ashpenaz be angry. Will tell the king."

The girl walked on, and Daniel watched her, while enthusiastically tearing open a pomegranate. She turned, nervously, and smiled back at him.

Suddenly, Daniel found himself remembering his old school, and his old teacher. As Daniel watched the slave girl, he thanked God for his school and his teacher.

"God is always there," the teacher had said, as Daniel was escorted away by Babylonian soldiers. "You cannot see God, but he always hears. Talk to him Daniel, and listen to him." Daniel's teacher had run after him and shouted to him, "God always talks to us, Daniel, listen to him."

Those were the last words that Daniel had heard in his own language. They were the last loving or caring words that had been said to him, until the whispered warning from the fruit girl. A single tear escaped from his eye and crawled down his cheek.

In the lonely silence, fruit in hand, Daniel followed his teacher's advice. "God of Heaven," he mouthed into his pomegranate so no one could see, "should I follow the ways of my own people, or must I become a Babylonian?"

He listened for an answer. He could hear the clank of silver dishes. He could hear the distant tap of the steward's cane. But he could not hear God.

He did, however, remember his father's voice, saying, "God does not give us rules to make us poor, Daniel, but to make us rich."

Some students were rising from their cushions, and gathering in friendly clusters. This was his chance. Daniel quickly pushed his dish aside and headed for the student he thought was a fellow Jew.

He introduced himself nervously, using the language of Babylon.

"You new?"

The other nodded.

"I'm from Jerusalem," Daniel said.

The other looked anxiously up and down the palace corridor. "Bethlehem," he said.

"I'm Daniel."

"My name is Azariah." Then a shadow seemed to fall across his face. "But Ashpenaz calls me Abednego."

"How long have you been here?" Daniel asked.

"Ten days," Azariah said, as if that were an entire lifetime.

"Is the food always like this?"

Azariah glanced down at the five eyeballs stranded at the bottom of his dish. "This is the worst," he said secretively, in Hebrew. Then he added mournfully, "Ashpenaz will make us eat it."

One of the palace guards was walking past. Daniel carefully positioned himself in front of the uneaten food. Azariah added, pointedly and in Babylonian, "Our food comes from the king. To refuse the food is to insult the king."

The two students looked miserably down at the eyeballs. "To eat it, however..." Daniel paused while another guard strode past, "is to insult our nation, and our God."

Azariah looked up, surprised by the mention of God.

"Which is worse?" Daniel asked him. "To insult the King of Babylon, or to insult the King of Heaven?"

"What about Ashpenaz?" Azariah asked, hopelessly.

"Who is this Ashpenaz?"

"The Chief Steward, the one with the cane."

Daniel nodded, "We must talk to him."

* * *

The four young Jews ran through the maze of dark corridors together. They didn't know where they were going, but for the moment they didn't care. They had escaped from the queasy stare of those wretched eyeballs. Hananiah was from Jerusalem too; Mishael from the little village of Bethany. They had all been chosen for the king's school. They were looking for Ashpenaz. They wanted to find him before he found them and forced them to eat the food. But they had no idea where he was.

"Are we allowed in this part of the palace?" Daniel asked his new friends.

"The basic rule," explained Mishael, who had been in Babylon the longest, "is that you never go through a closed door without permission."

"The second rule," Hananiah added darkly, "is that you never upset Ashpenaz."

They heard the sound of marching feet, and slowed down to an impatient walk. Daniel wanted to run – he had not been allowed to run for six weeks and it felt so good to be free to do so. Some soldiers passed without even looking at them. Daniel sprinted ahead as soon as they were out of sight. "Give us some help, God," he prayed quickly. The four of them ran, left and right, round and round, frantic, excited and scared.

"Stop!" Daniel shouted breathlessly. "I saw something."

He retraced his steps and craned his neck to look round a doorway, trying not to be seen. There she was – the fruit girl – squatting on a dirty floor, eating scraps from other people's dishes. There were other slaves in the same room.

Daniel coughed quietly, to attract her attention.

She looked up, straight into his eyes, and smiled. He beckoned her over. She looked cautiously around and slipped silently into the corridor.

"Where is Ashpenaz?" Daniel whispered.

She looked confused.

"I need to speak to Ashpenaz. Where is he?"

She looked at him with questioning caution. "Why would you want to talk to Ashpenaz?" her face asked.

"It's about the food," Daniel explained.

She seemed to understand.

"Ashpenaz – where can I find him?" he asked again.

Azariah, Hananiah and Mishael had joined him. The girl looked at them uncertainly.

"Friends," Daniel said simply. He knew that the girl spoke even less Babylonian than him.

She suddenly grabbed his hand and set off at a brisk walk, back in the direction from which they had come. The others followed.

"Where do you come from?" Daniel asked, while trying to free his hand from her grip.

"Shh!" she replied, holding on firmly.

They continued in cautious silence. Now that he was not running, Daniel began to consider what he might say to the chief steward when they found him. He had no ideas.

They heard muffled voices approaching and the girl darted through a closed door. Daniel was already in danger of breaking the second rule: don't upset Ashpenaz. He was reluctant to break the first by entering a closed room. But there was no time to think and the girl was still gripping his hand. The room was empty. Relief. No, it wasn't. There was an old woman in the corner. She looked up from her work, then looked down again. She had no interest in four young students and a slave girl.

The girl listened at the door. As the voices passed her eyes widened. She whispered, "The king."

Daniel was glad to be out of the corridor. His heart was pounding.

The king was a man he did not wish to meet. The king was the man who had ordered the total destruction of Jerusalem. He was also a man who considered stewed eyeballs a delicacy.

The voices faded. The girl opened the door and led them on. Around two more corners, she stopped, and pointed to a closed door. "Ashpenaz," she said. Then she released Daniel's hand.

He had wanted her to let go all along, but now he held on for a moment longer and said, "Thank you."

She bowed slightly and left, again walking swiftly, but not daring to run.

Daniel turned and faced the closed door. There were voices inside. He knocked. Nothing happened. He knocked louder. The voices went silent, someone laughed, and the voices began again.

"Perhaps they don't knock on doors like we do," Hananiah suggested.

Daniel placed his hand on the door latch. He would have to risk breaking basic rule number one. He deliberately remembered the sight and smell of the stewed eyeballs. It was worth the risk. He didn't want to face those again. He looked at Mishael who had told him about the closed door rule. Mishael was tense.

Daniel took his hand off the door latch. Then he prayed, this time loud enough for his friends to hear. "God, if you want us to live by your laws, you will have to help us – right now." He paused, looked around at his friends and added, "Amen."

The others muttered their own "Amen", and Daniel opened the door. Three proud-faced stewards stared up at him, but Ashpenaz was not there.

* * *

The next ten days passed quickly. Daniel was busy learning both the customs and the corridors of the royal palace. Every morning he, and his three friends, reported to Ashpenaz for their lessons in Babylonian language and literature.

Every morning, before the lesson began, Ashpenaz made them stand by the window, one at a time, while he closely examined their eyes, mouths and faces.

Ten day's earlier, it had seemed that there was no alternative to eating the king's food. The stewards had insisted, "If the king sees you looking pale and thin because you are not eating his food..." One of them drew his cane morbidly across the front of his neck.

At that moment, an idea had popped into Daniel's head. Did it come from God? He didn't know. "Give us ten days," he said politely but firmly. "Let us eat only vegetables and drink only water for ten days. Then compare us with the students who eat the royal food and make your decision, depending on what you see."

For those ten days, Daniel had received extra visits from the fruit girl every meal time. She always took her time in portioning out his helpings of vegetables and fruit. While she did, Daniel told her about the things he had seen on his daily tours of the vast city beyond the palace walls: about temples and elephants, markets and mountains.

Every day she asked Daniel the same question: "Did you see people from my country? Did you see anyone with my skin?"

Today was the tenth day. Today there would be no tour of the city. Today, Daniel, Azariah, Hananiah and Mishael had an appointment with the king's physician, to decide if they were more or less healthy than the other students.

The four friends were led by Ashpenaz through doors that had always been closed to them. They passed through royal apartments with thick carpets and gold furniture. At one point, Daniel thought he caught a glimpse of the queen, but he was not sure.

"In three years' time," Ashpenaz informed them, "if you continue with your studies, you will become advisers to the king, and you will visit these rooms every day."

At that moment the old steward stopped in his tracks and bent his long, lean back into a deep bow. "Lie down, on your faces," he spat at his four students. "Don't look up."

The urgency of his command was obvious. Daniel threw himself to the floor, pressing his nose into the deep woollen rug. He could see nothing but a blur of deep blue. He heard nothing either. A few moments later, Ashpenaz's cane prodded his neck.

"Get up," he whispered coarsely. "It was the king."

Daniel was not entirely sure that this was true. He looked closely at the steward's eyes, searching for a clue. The man turned away and paced off with long, measured strides.

Eventually they came to the royal physician's apartment. Inside, four of their fellow students were already standing in a strict row, wearing only their undergarments. Behind a table, by the window, sat a small fat man.

"If that belly is his measure of good heath," Hananiah whispered to Daniel, "we have no hope."

"Silence!" the man squawked, in an unusually high-pitched voice.

Daniel glared at Hananiah. Their future depended on a favourable report from this man. They could not afford to upset him.

"Undress!" the physician snapped, pushing himself to his feet.

The man strutted to the nearest student – one of the others. He rolled back the young man's eyelids, poked in his ears, stroked his hair, studied his teeth, squeezed his muscles. All the while he muttered to himself. Then, without warning, he punched the student sharply in the stomach. The young man groaned. The doctor smiled and moved on to the next. He punched the second student halfway through his examination. The third student was punched at the very beginning. The fourth tensed up for a fake strike but doubled up in pain when the real one was delivered.

Next it was the turn of the four Jews. Daniel would be the last. They had the advantage of knowing that the fat man was going to hit them, but Azariah, Hananiah and Mishael were all caught off guard. The physician was clearly enjoying this sport. Ashpenaz watched in silence.

Finally the doctor came to Daniel. Daniel's heart fluttered in his chest. He watched the physican's eyes, waiting for the slightest hint that he was about to strike. The doctor leaned close to inspect Daniel's eyes, his left hand holding Daniel's eyelid wide open. Daniel noticed a faint twitch in the man's face. His reactions were fast, he pulled his own left hand sharply up and grabbed on to the physician's wrist. The man smiled his congratulations at Daniel and relaxed. But Daniel did not. Moments later he spotted a fragment of tension in the man's cheek. He grasped the wrist as it returned for a second strike. This time the man stepped back. Daniel still did not allow himself to relax until the doctor was safely seated behind his table.

The physician looked steadily at each of the eight young men and then looked down at a sheet of papyrus on his table.

"Four have been eating the royal diet, and four only vegetables," he said, half questioning, half stating the fact.

"That is correct," Ashpenaz replied stiffly.

"It is easy to tell which is which," the doctor smiled smugly.

Daniel's heart sank. He had prayed to God every mealtime for ten days, and so had Azariah, Hananiah, and Mishael.

"I advise the king on what is good to eat," the physician continued, his voice thick with pride. "And what is good for the king is good for you." He glared at all eight of them.

Daniel was praying frantically. Was it ever too late to pray? He didn't know.

"I insist," the physician stabbed out the words, "that you eat what I choose," he was still looking down, "or I shall see to it that the king has you disembowelled in public."

Daniel felt a sudden pain in his belly.

"You," he continued, walking up to the four students who had been eating the king's food, "must stop your silly nonsense." The four blinked in surprise. "Whereas you," he waddled towards the four young Jews with a sickly smile, "are the healthiest young men I have seen in many years." He scowled at Ashpenaz and returned to his desk.

Ashpenaz did not move, unsure whether or not to point out the physician's mistake. He tapped the floor nervously with his cane. The physician looked up at him and said, "Are you still here?"

"You four," Ashpenaz barked at the students who had arrived first, "go to your rooms. I will see you later." The students picked up their clothes uncertainly and shuffled out. "You four," he said more softly to Daniel and his friends, "have done... very well." He shifted uneasily, aware that the king's physician was watching him. "It... it would seem, that... that you know what's good for you."

An impatient sigh came from behind the table.

Ashpenaz, who had his back to the physician, allowed a smile to creep across his face. "You may continue."

* * *

God gave the four young Jews knowledge and understanding in all their learning, and none of the other students were equal to them.

This story is taken from the Bible, from chapter 1 of the book of Daniel (that's in the Old Testament). Why not get hold of a Bible and read more about Daniel, Azariah, Hananiah and Mishael in Daniel chapters 1 to 6? Read about giant statues, disembodied hands, fiery furnaces and lions' dens, but God is always in control.

Books from Scripture Union

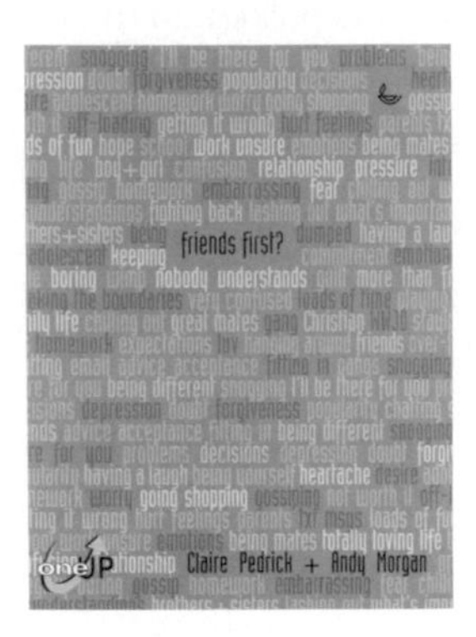

Friends First

Claire Pedrick and Andy Morgan

Friends First takes a look at relationships and how confusing they can get: friendship groups, girlfriends, best friends, boyfriends and even being friends with your parents! This book helps you untangle these relationships. Peer pressure, flirting, going to church and what to do about bullying are all covered in this extremely useful book!

1 85999 644 2

£3.99

Under Pressure

Claire Pedrick and Andy Morgan

Get some help from this fantastic new handbook on how to deal with the stuff that gives you stress and puts you under pressure. From exams to friends, from parents to the outside world, stress comes from everywhere. Get some valuable advice on how to stop it squeezing you!

1 84427 008 4

£3.99

These books and many more are available from your local Christian bookshop or from Scripture Union Mail Order: 0845 07 06 006 or www.scriptureunion.org.uk/shop

(Prices are correct at the time of going to press)

My teacher

My teacher My teacher My teacher

My teacher once wore nappies
My teacher used to crawl
My teacher used to cry at night
My teacher used to bawl.

My teacher jibber jabbered
My teacher ran up stairs
My teacher wrote in squiggles
My teacher stood on chairs.

My teacher once was naughty
My teacher was so rude
My teacher used a bad word
My teacher spilled her food.

My teacher lost her homework
My teacher took too long
My teacher got detention
My teacher did things wrong.

My teacher's all grown-up now
My teacher can't recall
My teacher thinks she's different
My teacher's not at all.

It's your move groove

Now this is a story about an ordinary guy
Whose small school life had passed him by.
He had had a great time – life full of tricks,
But now it-was-the-end! Bye-bye Year 6!

When the time came, he'd not know how he'd feel
To be a very small cog in a very big wheel.
He'd... not... know – what... it was to be,
Just a very small fish in a very big sea.

Mooooooviiiing – it's a bit scary,
It's a bit new.
Moooooviing – just remember,
To be YOU!

Moving

September was here and it started bad.
The place was big – timetable mad.
He found he'd be lost when the bell would ring
And the stairs seemed to move like the Harry Potter thing.

But after a while, he got to know
To join in, chill out – and go with the flow.
He'd no longer worry about the pain in the neck
When Year-12s came by, even bigger than Shrek.

Moooooviiiing – it's a bit scary,
It's a bit new.
Moooooviing – just remember,
To be YOU!

Half term soon came and he'd have to say
He could still remember that scary first day,
But he had his new friends and new things to do
And even the teachers were quite human too.

Moooooviiiing – it's a bit scary,
It's a bit new.
Moooooviing – just remember,
To be YOU!

Just remember – TO BE YOU

Bob Miles

When it all gets too much!

If, after reading everything in this book, you're still feeling a bit stressed, here's a page which will give you a bit of light relief!

There were two snakes.
One said to the other,
"Hey, are we poisonous?"
"No," he said.
"That's a relief," said the first,
"I've just bitten my lip".

What did the plant that sat in the Maths lesson grow?
Square roots!

Why didn't the polar bear eat the penguin?
He couldn't get the wrapper off!

Mother zebra to baby zebra:
"No dear, we can't afford a new Arsenal strip. You'll just have to support Newcastle like the rest of us!"

Teacher: Hands up anyone who can tell me the name of the first woman on earth. I'll give you a clue: apples.
Alec: Was it Granny Smith, miss?

Treble-decker sandwich

Get home from your first day, starving! Want something to celebrate? Something a bit different? Try this treble-decker sandwich! ...

You will need:

Three slices of bread
(brown or white to suit!)
Butter or margarine
Fillings: jam, cheese, lettuce, ham, peanut butter, sliced tomatoes, cucumber, crisps, bacon (cooked), mayonnaise, ketchup, tuna, lemon curd, pickle!
Sharp knife

All you need to do:

Choose your two favourite fillings.
Spread butter or margarine on the bread.
Put one filling on the bottom layer.
Cover with a slice of bread.
Put second filling on top.
Place slice of bread on top.
Cut in half.

Eat with care! Enjoy!

The It's Your Move!

Holiday!

Moving on to any new situation can be quite scary. To meet up with others facing the same challenge can make it seem a lot less difficult. That's why a crowd of nearly twenty young people, who were going to move on to secondary school in six weeks time, went on a holiday for three days and two nights. They had a brilliant time canoeing and raft-building, abseiling and climbing high ropes, building camp fires and playing weird, wild and wacky games. They discovered the adventures of characters in the Bible who moved onto new things PLUS the bonus of sharing with others who were also preparing for 'moving on up'. Their leaders listened, talked, laughed and gave them some wise advice. More holidays are planned for this summer.

One parent said of the It's Your Move! holiday, "Ruth had a great time. Her only complaint was that it was so short." One girl said, "Brilliant fun! It really helped me get ready for secondary school."

For details, contact
www.scriptureunion.org.uk/holidays or
holidays@scriptureunion.org.uk or
01908 856000

I'll miss the teacher with red hair!

I go to Mellor Primary School in Leicester. I think I will miss Mellor quite a lot, as I have been there almost all my life. I will miss all my teachers and my friends that are not going to my secondary school. I think I will be OK moving to a new school. We have started to move classes for different lessons but nowhere near as many as we'll have to at secondary school.

I am looking forward to meeting new friends. At Mellor, I will miss my teachers and my friends, but most of all the funny things like when my teacher Jon was running and he slipped over. Or when he dyed his hair red. Another thing I will miss is calling the teachers by their first names.

Before I leave Mellor, I am going to make an autograph book in which I will have as many signatures as possible so I will have a memory of everyone.

From the Scottish islands

A few weeks to go!

Hannah, Iain and Laura live on the Isle of Benbecula, in Western Scotland. They will be going to Sgoil Lionacleit (Liniclate Secondary) which is nearly six kilometres along the coast road from where they live. In the summer term they spent an induction week in the school.

Hannah Beattie has been to four primary schools, so she is used to being a new girl. She looks forward to having different subjects and teachers throughout the day. She isn't looking forward to getting up 45 minutes earlier to catch the bus! Iain MacVicar has an older brother at Sgoil Lionacleit. He knows what to expect. He will miss being just five minutes away from home, but looks forward to the wide selection of food in the school cafeteria. Iain thought that knowing Jesus would be important if he got bullied because Jesus would know what was going on even if other people didn't believe him.

Laura Whittaker has Down's syndrome and she has a learning support assistant with her all the time. She'll need lots of help at first to get used to her new school. She enjoyed the induction week and after the second day, she was able to go to the bus stop on her own. She made a new friend, a boy who has similar difficulties. She is looking forward to meeting him again and getting to know her other classmates.

Hannah Beattie

Iain MacVicar

Laura Whittaker

The coolest bit of the uniform is the TRACKSUIT!

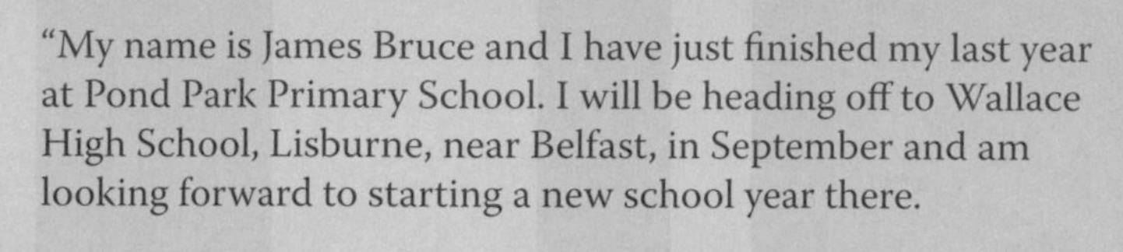

"My name is James Bruce and I have just finished my last year at Pond Park Primary School. I will be heading off to Wallace High School, Lisburne, near Belfast, in September and am looking forward to starting a new school year there.

What I am most looking forward to is meeting new people and doing new things like Food Technology, Biology, Technology and other stuff that I haven't done before. I'm scared of being the smallest in the school again – in case I get bullied – but I hope that won't happen. There will only be one other person from my primary school in my new class, so I guess I'll have to make some new friends.

The uniform makes me feel like I'm going to work in an office. I've got to wear a tie with house colours on it which I don't suppose I'll wear anywhere else really. I am a Christian, so I'll ask God to help me not be scared."

We're not allowed to wear jeans!

Sheryn Macintosh

"I'm going to Yardley School in Birmingham," says Sheryn Macintosh.
"The uniform is a green jumper, black or green trousers or skirt and a white shirt. The shoes we wear are loafers.

I feel excited and very sad because
I am going to leave all my friends behind.
But my personality is cheerful, outgoing and determined so I'm looking forward to meeting new friends. I will miss all the extra days off and being able to go off to the loo during lesson times. Changing school is a big challenge but I feel I can trust God in everything I do!"

Rebekah Muir (11) goes to Lairdsland Primary, Kirkintilloch near Glasgow. She is really looking forward to starting at Lenzie Academy after the summer. She says, "I moved school two years ago and I was a bit worried then about making friends. But I needn't have worried because I quickly made friends with Rosie and Alexandrea who were put in my work-group!" Rosie and Alexandrea will be moving up with Rebekah, and her big sister is already at the school.

I needn't have worried because I quickly made friends

Rebekah enjoys gymnastics, playing the recorder and flute, and loves to draw cartoons. "I am a 'Buddy' to three Primary-1s and that's a bit scary, but I do enjoy being one of the older ones. We have a Scripture Union group in our school every Thursday – it's fun, and sometimes I bring my friends. We hear stories from the Bible and discover just how much God loves us.

"I'm a bit worried about going to Lenzie Academy, which has over 1,300 students. I'll be starting at the bottom again! I'm a bit worried about all the work I'll have to do, but because I know God helped me when I moved before, I know I needn't worry and can trust him to be with me in the future! I'm looking forward to art and technology classes and to seeing what clubs I might join. I know there is an SU group and I'm looking forward to being a part of that."

So many different things!

Maybe you have been used to going to quite a small school and are now moving to a school that is much bigger. That was my experience and I can tell you, it was a bit of a shock to the system. More children, more teachers and more of everything. One way of avoiding frustrations and anxious feelings is to make sure that you arrive at the right classroom for every lesson. This was hard work for me during the first few days of year 7. One example was when I had an English lesson. I found myself in an English classroom but with the wrong teacher. I quickly learnt that there were many different things in secondary school, not only more teachers, but even more than one teacher for each subject. A map would have been useful during those first few days. I would also have appreciated a fuller introduction to the layout of the school and being told exactly where all the toilets were!

Robin Williams age 12

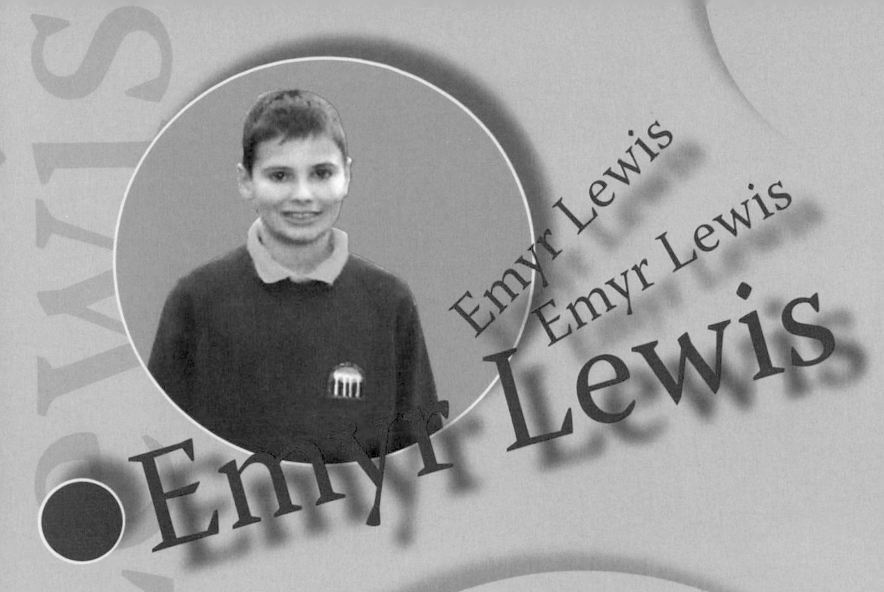

Hi, my name's Emyr Lewis, and I've just started at Ysgol Bro Morgannwg in South Wales. All the lessons are in Welsh and I was a bit worried because I'm the only Welsh speaker in my family and I didn't think I would have any help with homework. But the teachers have been brilliant! They are always there to help.

I was also a bit nervous about catching the school bus. People kept telling me that older pupils throw things like rotten apples at you. But they didn't, and I soon made new friends on the bus. I made lots of new friends in my classes as well. My tip for enjoying school is: Make new friends as quickly as you can – and let them help you if you're having problems with anything.

The school was nothing like I expected. It was like my old school – just bigger, with a few more facilities, like tennis and basketball courts. We've had some really exciting lessons already. In technology we've been making juggling balls! The teachers are cool, too. Sometimes they're strict, but they're always fair!

My mum teaches there!!

"Hi! My name is Hannah Smith and I am 12 years old and go to Watford School for Girls. When you start at a new school you don't know everyone so you have to make friends. I didn't have any problems making friends but on the first day I didn't know anyone in my form.

My mum teaches RS at the school and is Head of Year 11. Two of my friends have mothers working there too! I think it is fun having a mum as a teacher because she knows what I am doing during exams and also knows my teachers well. If I ever need anything, I can go and see her.

My school offers a lot to the pupils and I enjoy going to Fencing one lunch-time a week. My school is huge and I kept getting lost in the first week, even though I had been there with my mum when I was younger.

My advice to anyone changing schools is: don't get upset about going to another school as it is fun and you can still keep in touch with your old friends."

What to take on your first day

Rachel Anderson goes to St Joan of Arc Roman Catholic School, in Rickmansworth. This is what she advises you to take on your first day: "A pencil case containing a pencil, pen, ruler, rubber, sharpener and ink eraser, plus lunch (or money to buy your lunch) and paper, both lined and plain. The teachers will tell you about anything else you'll need."
And she's got some good advice about homework: "You will get a lot of homework so it's better to get it done the night you get it. Then you get the weekend free to relax."

I didn't get my first choice

Karl Hemingway had to take an entrance exam to decide which secondary school he would go to. He was nervous before the exam but he talked with God and that helped him. However, he was very disappointed when he didn't get into his first choice school. However, he says,

"I am now glad I went to Rickmansworth School and I wonder why I worried so much."

When I was moving school I felt nervous and excited at the same time. There are lots of changes when you move to secondary school, like the way you have more than one teacher and how much stricter they are. The tasks you are asked to do are much harder and you get a lot of homework. But you are respected more and there many more facilities."

His advice is: "Look at it like this – going to secondary school is like a big adventure just waiting for you."

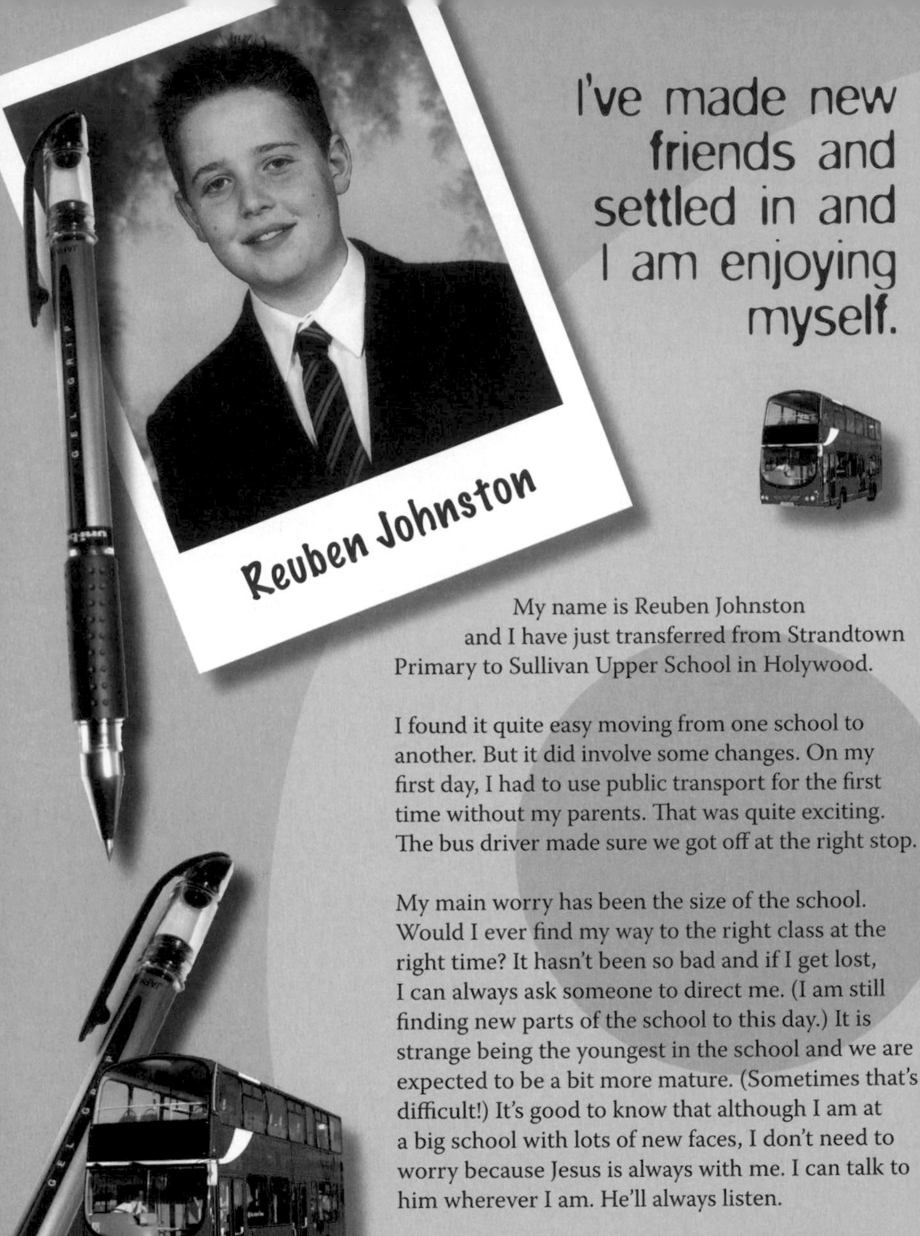

I've made new friends and settled in and I am enjoying myself.

My name is Reuben Johnston and I have just transferred from Strandtown Primary to Sullivan Upper School in Holywood.

I found it quite easy moving from one school to another. But it did involve some changes. On my first day, I had to use public transport for the first time without my parents. That was quite exciting. The bus driver made sure we got off at the right stop.

My main worry has been the size of the school. Would I ever find my way to the right class at the right time? It hasn't been so bad and if I get lost, I can always ask someone to direct me. (I am still finding new parts of the school to this day.) It is strange being the youngest in the school and we are expected to be a bit more mature. (Sometimes that's difficult!) It's good to know that although I am at a big school with lots of new faces, I don't need to worry because Jesus is always with me. I can talk to him wherever I am. He'll always listen.

Now that I have been at Sullivan for a while, I have made new friends and settled in and am enjoying myself.

In the spotlight

Year 7 tutor (Guidance teacher)

Name: David Weeks
Age: Middle-aged
School: Chosen Hill Comprehensive School, Churchdown, Gloucestershire
Subject: Geography
Likes: Gliding, ballooning and surfing
Fave food: Strawberries and cream – reminds me of summer days!

Worst classroom experience

Telling a pupil to stop banging his desk. 'It's an earthquake, Sir!' he said. And he was right!

Words of wisdom

Don't believe the horror stories of heads being flushed down loos. They are not true!

Top teacher tips

- Make sure you are organised. Then life will be easier for you and everyone else.
- Never be afraid to ask for help, and talk to someone you can trust before problems get worse.

Assemblies

I ask God for help when I have to do a scary assembly in front of two hundred pupils. He also gives me the right words to say when I'm talking with someone about bullying or misunderstandings at home. This year in assemblies I talked about street children. Pupils were so concerned, they wanted to know what could be done. We talked about how important it is to know that God cares for everyone, including street children.

Last words

Always make an effort to make new friends. Don't just stick with the old ones.

In the spotlight

Form Tutor (Guidance teacher)

Name: Alison Woodward
Age: 30
School: St Paul's Roman Catholic School, Milton Keynes
Subject: Italian and French. Currently a Year 10 form tutor too
Fave Food: Pasta with anything (well, nearly!)
Likes: Hockey, skiing, travelling

My first day at secondary school

I had a nice new uniform (including trendy navy-blue tank top) and a VERY large bag! I expected secondary school to be just like *Grange Hill* on TV and I remember being disappointed that my school didn't have any stairs.

Words of wisdom

Tutors or teachers do actually want to help you settle in – they don't just shout for the sake of it!

Make the effort to speak to the other people in your form group and in other classes. Don't just hang around with those from your previous school. Also, be aware of other students who may have just moved to the area and do not know anybody – make sure you include them.

What not to do!

Make sure you know what you need for the first day. However, you don't have to buy brand new trainers, every type of pen available, all the latest software packages, a new computer, the whole of W H Smith, etc...

First impressions last a long time, so make sure yours are good for organisation, presentation and behaviour. Your aim should not be to establish yourself as the toughest, roughest, loudest member of the year group!

Top teacher tips

This is your chance to make a fresh start – make a stand for what you know is right. Make the most of new opportunities. Go along to clubs and try out new activities.

Don't forget!

There are many people you can turn to for help or for a chat. Remember that God is one of them. I often pray as I drive to work (with my eyes open, I must add!) to ask for his strength and help.

Induction checklist

When you visit your new school there are some key things to do:

1. Make notes and write down everything you need to remember.
2. Behave in a way that won't get you noticed too quickly.
3. Try to get to know one or two other pupils in your new form.
4. Find out about ...
   - the layout of the school
   - where the toilets are
   - your timetable
   - the uniform
   - the time you should arrive each morning

If these issues aren't raised, ask questions to make sure you know all you need to know.

checklist

checklist

checklist

Homework timetable

Monday	
Tuesday	
Wednesday	
Thursday	
Friday	

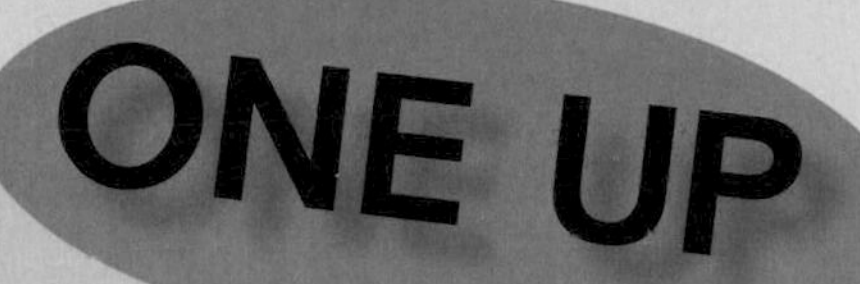

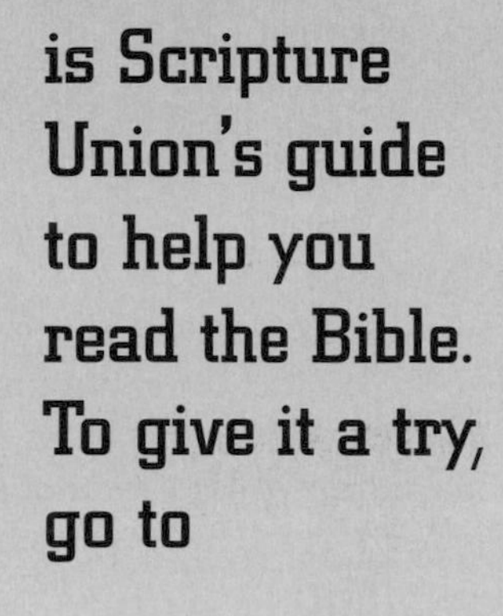

is Scripture Union's guide to help you read the Bible. To give it a try, go to

www.scriptureunion.org.uk/oneup

Answer from page 6: The Bible is the world's best-selling book. Over 500 million Bibles or extracts of the Bible are distributed worldwide every year!

Scripture Union is an international Christian charity working in more than 130 countries. Christians believe that their faith in Jesus is important and affects how they live their lives every day. So Scripture Union employs and supports schools workers in local schools to lead assemblies, take RE lessons and act as a listening ear to students of all ages. Scripture Union runs holidays and camps for children and young people and publishes books for young people, including *One Up* (see below). If you'd like to find out what Christians believe, or more about the work of Scripture Union contact the address below or check out the website on www.scriptureunion.org.uk.

England and Wales: Scripture Union, 207–209 Queensway, Bletchley, Milton Keynes, England, MK2 2EB. Tel: 01908 856000

Northern Ireland: Scripture Union, 157 Albertbridge Road, Belfast, Northern Ireland, BT5 4PS. Tel: 028 9045 4806

Republic of Ireland: Scripture Union, 87 Lower George's Street, Dun Laoghaire Co, Dublin, Irish Republic. Tel: 01 280 2300

Scotland: Scripture Union, 70 Milton Street, Glasgow, Scotland, G4 0HR. Tel: 0141 332 1162

Nick's Last Words for Survival

1 Preparation

Make sure you take all the equipment you need every day (the My Little Pony lunchbox you had at primary school may need updating!). Have a notebook to jot down important info about school. Check your travel arrangements – walking, cycling, car, bus, helicopter – **BE SAFE.**

2 Punctuality

Arrive on time every morning (preferably alert after a good night's sleep). Carry a timetable with you at all times so you know which class you're supposed to be in and when. This will avoid major embarrassment!

3 Perspective

Secondary school isn't really a 'wild jungle' – more like a zoo with lots of interesting animals, so don't hide behind the friends you already know; make some new ones. The zoo keepers are there to help you, not just to contain you – don't be afraid to ask if you need anything. Beware, there are a few dangerous species (but even they are in cages!).

Nick Jeffery spent three years as a Community Worker with the Royal Navy. He has 12 years of experience as a Christian schools worker. He now sets up projects with the local authority to support pupils who are in their first year at secondary school. He is married with three children and is a mad supporter of Portsmouth Football Club!